TREASURE HUNT!

Sean Callery

Crabtree Publishing Company
www.crabtreebooks.com

Author: Sean Callery
Editors: Kathy Middleton
Crystal Sikkens
Project coordinator: Kathy Middleton
Production coordinator: Ken Wright
Prepress technicians: Ken Wright
Margaret Amy Salter

Picture Credits:
Dreamstime: Erik Gauger: page 10; Witold Krasowski: page 18; Mitja Mladkovic: pages 1, 5 (top)
Shutterstock: cover; Alfredolon: page 21; Galina Barskaya: page 4; Bobby Deal/RealDealPhoto: page 13; Eric Gevaert: page 19; Fer Gregory: page 12; Anna Jurkovska: page 16; Eduard Kyslynskyy: page 11; Myotis: page 15; Lobke Peers: page 8; Sakala: page 6; Jozef Sedmak: page 9; Dani Simmonds: page 14; Zoran Vukmanov Simokov: page 7; Sandra van der Steen: page 17; Tatjana Strelkova: pages 3, 20; SueC: page 5 (bottom)

Library and Archives Canada Cataloguing in Publication

Callery, Sean
Treasure hunt / Sean Callery.

(Crabtree connections)
Includes index.
ISBN 978-0-7787-7852-3 (bound).--ISBN 978-0-7787-7874-5 (pbk.)

1. Pirates--Juvenile literature. 2. Treasure troves--Juvenile literature. I. Title. II. Series: Crabtree connections

G535.C34 2011   j910.4'5   C2011-900613-8

Library of Congress Cataloging-in-Publication Data

Callery, Sean.
Treasure hunt / Sean Callery.
p. cm. -- (Crabtree connections)
Includes index.
ISBN 978-0-7787-7874-5 (pbk. : alk. paper) --
ISBN 978-0-7787-7852-3 (reinforced library binding : alk. paper)
1. Pirates--Juvenile literature. 2. Treasure troves--Juvenile literature. I. Title.
G535.C28 2011
910.4'5--dc22
                                        2011001355

Crabtree Publishing Company
www.crabtreebooks.com   1-800-387-7650
Copyright © 2012 **CRABTREE PUBLISHING COMPANY.**
All rights reserved. No part of this publication may be reproduced, stored in a retrieval system or be transmitted in any form or by any means, electronic, mechanical, photocopying, recording, or otherwise, without the prior written permission of Crabtree Publishing Company. Published in the United Kingdom in 2011 by A & C Black Publishers Ltd. The right of the author of this work has been asserted.

Printed in the U.S.A./072011/WO20110114

Published in Canada
Crabtree Publishing
616 Welland Ave.
St. Catharines, Ontario
L2M 5V6

Published in the United States
Crabtree Publishing
PMB 59051
350 Fifth Avenue, 59th Floor
New York, New York 10118

Contents

Hop On Board

I am **Captain** Black. This is the story of one of my greatest treasure hunts ever.

Look at that ship!
One day at sea, I spotted a huge ship. "Raise the Jolly Roger!" I shouted.

I told my **crew** to attack.

We'll fight you

The Jolly Roger was a pirate **flag**. It was a signal to other ships that the **pirates** would fight.

Attack!

There was no treasure on the big ship. But we did find a **treasure map**—hurrah!

Take it all

We didn't take just the map. We stole the ship too!

Give me your ship!

We pirates were great fighters.

Treasure hunters

Pirates hunted for treasure such as jewels, gold, and silver.

treasure

Treasure!

The treasure map showed an island. It was marked with an X—for treasure.

Let's go

"There's **loot** there!" I told my crew. We **voted** to sail for the island right away.

Treasure maps were drawn by hand.

Hands up

Pirates voted by raising their hands if they agreed.

X marks the spot.

Danger Island

Then we sailed to the island. As we waded to the shore, a crocodile bit me on the leg.

Cook and doctor

Our cook patched up my leg. Pirate cooks didn't just cook— they were the ships' doctors too.

Look out for crocs!

Don't go in the water

Pirates had to watch out for a lot of dangerous sea creatures.

A perfect treasure island

Dig, Me Hearties!

Next we reached the spot marked X on the map. "Dig!" I shouted to my pirate crew.

Found it!

As we dug, our shovels hit something hard. Then we saw a wooden chest. I knew the treasure must be inside.

Pirates hid their treasure in chests.

We're all rich

Pirates always shared treasure. But the captain got the most!

treasure chest

What is inside?

Lovely Loot

Bang! Joe fired his **pistol** at the lock, and it snapped open. The chest was full of coins.

Money, money, money

Inside the chest we saw lots of gold coins. They were called **doubloons**.

Treasure

doubloon

Cut-up coins

Silver coins that could be cut up to share were called "pieces of eight."

Never come between a pirate and his treasure!

Over Here!

Then Ben lit a bonfire so our **shipmates** still on the ship could see where we were.

No cell phones...

We pirates didn't have phones or radios. We used flags, fires, and even trumpets to send messages.

bonfire ————————○

I can see you

Pirates did have **telescopes**. This tool helped them to see things far away.

This way →

Our shipmates rowed ashore to meet us.

Load Up

We filled the boat with treasure. Ben said he would row it back to the ship. He promised to come back for us.

A pirate's life

We all needed that treasure. Once you are a pirate, you can't get an honest job!

Ben took the treasure back to our ship.

Pirate pets

Although pirates were tough, they still kept pets, such as monkeys.

See you!

The End?

Can you believe it? Ben sailed away without us. Arghhhh!

Island life

We were left alone on the island, with no ship and no treasure. Ben had taken the whole thing.

Pirates fought to the death for treasure.

20

We'll get him

If we ever catch Ben, we'll dump him on an island. Hey, wait...that's just what he's done to us!

Just you wait, Ben!

Glossary

captain Person who is in charge of a ship and its crew

crew Pirates and sailors who work on a ship

doubloons Spanish gold coins

flag Piece of material with a pattern or picture

loot Money, jewels, or other things that pirates stole from ships

pirates Robbers who stole from ships

pistol Small gun

shipmates Sailors or pirates who belonged to the same crew

telescopes Tools that help people to see things far away

treasure map Drawing that showed pirates where to find loot

voted Chose

Further Reading

Web Sites

Read all about pirates, and try out some fun games at:
www.nationalgeographic.com/pirates

There is a lot of information about pirates at:
www.thekidswindow.co.uk/News/Pirates.htm

Books

Pirate by Deborah Lock, DK Children (2005).

Pirates: Rogues' Gallery by John Matthews, Summit Press (2007).

Why Did Pirates Bury Treasure? by Catherine Chambers, Miles Kelly (2010).

Index